About the Author

A Canadian poet from Iraqi origins who was born in 1942 in a village in the province of Mayson in southern Iraq. He completed his elementary school education at the local village school and later at the school of Al-Kumayt in the nearby village. He received a diploma in education from the college of education in 1963. He worked in the field of education, journalism and radio broadcasting between 1963 and 1990. In 2001 he arrived in Canada, where he resided in Winnipeg and then moved permanently to Montreal (Quebec). He is a member of « Union des écrivaines et des écrivains québécois » 2018 , « Quebec Writers' Federation» 2019, and the Union Writers of Canada 2012–2016

He received several awards including: "The Free Word" prize from Poets of All Nations (PAN) in 2002, during the "International Festival of Poetry" in Rotterdam, Netherlands, and the Phoenix International Prize, from Dar al-Qissa in Iraq, 2008, for his novel, "The Days of Muhssineh's village".

About the Translator

Emeritus Professor
Abdul Wahid Mohammed Muslat (PhD)

Professor Abdul Wahid Mohammed was born in 1933 in the Maysan Governate, Iraq. He served in the Ministry of Education as a secondary school teacher for twelve years and in the Ministry of Higher Education and scientific Research as a staff member for forty years. He worked as the head of the Department of English in the College of Languages at University of Baghdad and later as the dean of the same college. There, he supervised and discussed many theses and dissertations in linguistics and translation. He taught linguistics, discourse analysis, stylistics, translation theory and translation criticism at postgraduate level. He has translated twenty-five literary books, in addition to what he has published in journals. He translated four anthologies of Iraqi poetry into English: *Fatherhood*, by Adeeb Kamal Ad-Deen, published in Australia; *The Herb,* by Issa Hassan Al-Yasiri, published in Iraq; *Aphrodite,* by Mohammed Husain Al-Yaseen published in

Jordan; and ***They Die…He Doesn't***, short stories by Hanoon Majeed published in Iraq. In addition, he has translated numerous other poems for publication in newspapers and journals.

He has been interviewed on many occasions by the press. He obtained several approval certificates from different sources and has participated in several festivals and conferences, both local and internationally. His biography has been included in the first volume of the ***Encyclopedia of Iraqi Figures in the 20th century***, compiled by Hameed Al-Matba'i in Baghdad in 1995.

The Herb

Poetry

Issa Hassan Al-Yasiri

The Herb

Poetry

Translated by Emeritus Professor
Abdul Wahid Mohammed (PhD)

Edited by Elliot Montpellier

Olympia Publishers
London

www.olympiapublishers.com
OLYMPIA PAPERBACK EDITION

Copyright © Issa Hassan Al-Yasiri 2022

The right of Issa Hassan Al-Yasiri to be identified as author of this work has been asserted in accordance with sections 77 and 78 of the Copyright, Designs and Patents Act 1988.

All Rights Reserved

No reproduction, copy or transmission of this publication may be made without written permission.
No paragraph of this publication may be reproduced, copied or transmitted save with the written permission of the publisher, or in accordance with the provisions of the Copyright Act 1956 (as amended).

Any person who commits any unauthorised act in relation to this publication may be liable to criminal prosecution and civil claims for damage.

A CIP catalogue record for this title is available from the British Library.

ISBN: 978-1-80074-316-8

First Published in 2022

Olympia Publishers
Tallis House
2 Tallis Street
London
EC4Y 0AB

Printed in Great Britain

Dedication

Dedicated to the memory of the Australian poet Anne Fairbarin and Arab poet Ghazi Al — Gosaibi, who were the first to translate my poems into English and opened the door for readers of all walks of life to read my poetry.

Acknowledgements

Thanks, and appreciation to McGill University, which provided a financial grant to review the translation of the book "The Herb" on the initiative of Dr Rula Jurdi Abisaab and Dr Malek Abisaab, professors at the university.

Preface

I have been acquainted with Issa Hassan Al-Yasiri since the beginning of the sixties, at the time of teaching him English, then at the Primary Teacher Training School in Al-Amarah, the city seat of Maysan Governate in the South of Iraq. He often participated in the national celebrations and occasions by reciting metrical poems which have been frequently acclaimed by his listeners.

Years later he abandoned this type of poetry and started to practice writing the 'Prose Poem' in his own way until he became remarkably skillful in formalizing it and drawing its poetic images. By the passage of time, he could successfully achieve publishing seven books of poetry which attained a wide fame among the readers as well as a great appreciation by Iraqi and Arab critics.

Most of his poems are featured with transparency, freshness, elegance of themes, grace of images and boldness in posing incentive world issues. As he grew older and a lot of water passed under his bridge and his horizons of knowledge in poetry and culture enlarged, his poetic tools developed as well. He showed a clear inclination to what may be called 'a linguistic density' and a comprehensive poetic scene with a blend of local and universal elements. He also made use of the Iraqi folklore, the historical and mythical symbols, employing the technique of numerating his stanzas. This technique was a great aid to his poetic memory to wander about freely in the spaces of reality and imagination far away from all restrictions of time and place. By this technique, he could also construct graceful poetic clauses; characterized with appealing effect upon both the reader and the listener. One of the most remarkable specifications of his poetry is his fondness of widely using simile on which I formerly wrote a detailed study.

The 'village,' particularly the one in which he spent his earliest years, is thought of as the basic element in his poetry, in addition to the subject of woman, especially the woman whom he associates closely with or the one whom he discloses his love to before witnesses in nature like sparrows, larks, doves and shag, before trees such as willows, date-palms and vineyards and before sheep, goats and horses. He also does this before the rivers and brooklets where silence reigns and nothing sounds except the beats of two hearts soaring up away from the noise of modern cities which abound with the sounds of motors, wheels, cranes and even of the explosives and the mines of booby-trapped cars.

Oh, Issa! I see you, in this book of poetry, turn into a philosopher, a Sufi and a contemplator. Your village in the countryside of Al-Amara, too, has changed into a kind of utopia with a special attractive relish.

    Abdul Wahid Mohammed
    Baghdad
    21st May 2013

The Poem

How does the poem come out,
Without a revelatory woman
Who awakes the life
From the branch's tip
Down to the furthest roots?

A Moment of Love

She said,
While hiding her eyes into my chest,
This night has no flashing star.
Warm me, the chill of darkness
Horrifies me,
This fear trickles even from my sleeve.
Take me, perhaps I forget you
And forget,
My name,
I said,
While watching the withering lamp,
Don't be distressed if darkness
Has lasted long,
In the house
And the beloved has gone away
Look! Your eyes are telling me that
The dawn is behind the door.

I Name You A Dream

1
When the night becomes thick,
In the dimness of your eyes, I open
A window,
I peep through.
I see blue-roofed cities
And myself as a field,
Engendering evergreen trees
And birds without feathers of migration.

2
A vision, I call you.
It overtakes me
And slips away across the veins to
The body of
Earth,
Across the sky of exiles and
The river of
Memory.
Will you have a rest after the pathway,
Tiredness?
Will waters heading for the sea
Have a rest?
Oh, lady! I know you are as vast as
A labyrinth,

You are farther than what distances,
Cafes and times of cold
May assume.

3
Your grief was a little rivulet,
In which, as little kids, we waded.
It moistened our clothes
And left frail grass and epidemics
Upon our tiny faces.

4
Your grief grew larger when we
Became older.
I drew your grief in the form of man,
With feet cracked by crossing
Long distances,
Traveling to you,
So were the clouds,
Bearing the language of water,
And the bread of lovers,
And the trees receive the beats of axes
Thus, they bleed, but do not die.

5
A peg of concerns pressing the
Heart, I call you,
Or a shade I seek refuge in,
For the shadows above me have been torn asunder
And the dog days of summer have anguished me.
I name you, and name you a dream, and I…
Wake up.

The Desire

1
Between the clock and the wall,
I read your face.

2
This year's bag is
Stuffed with white papers and letters,
Unwritten yet:
My lady,
Does the dashing time await
This tired voice?

3
At midnight, the last bus leaves,
In the room I smash my glass
And invoke the last face that abandoned me.

4
Does my lady weep over papers
Falling down,
To the bottom of my heart?

5
How cold I feel tonight!

How much I dream of cities crowded
Inside you,
And of warm wine.

Awake

1
In your hair
Pure moons hide tonight
In you
r hair.
My heart hides tonight
My fingers
And all the years of my lifetime.

2
Did I tell you about the trees that bloomed in fire?
About a face that
Once loved you,
Then accompanied the rivers.

3
Nothing frightens the calm river,
Nothing can surprise this silence but you
When the last shadow may leave,
A visitor to all your seasons
And your love's fields, I remain.

4
Since many years,
I have known of no rivers that flow
As your
Hair's streamlets do,
I have known of no paths so green as your
Eyes are.

5
Across the desolate night's passages,
Through the woods of life, broken
Above the frenzied wind,
I sensed your presence
And sensed that ages of agony
Were retreating,
To make room for dawn.

6
Who has wakened me at this hour,
Of my death?
You?
Or a moon next to my home?

The Water Lilies

1
The flower has its own sadness;
The bird has its own favourite songs,
While I have the remnants of the
Village's dream,
When the brasier was blown out
Or when the wind was calling to the village.

2
He said to me,
Keeping an eye on the jammed street,
Wearing his bitter countenance,
"Painful are the seasons of migration."
I wept and he handed me some wine.

3
Since we have parted,
We still dream of the happy island.
Our dreams still keep traveling towards
A village, hidden
Under the shadows of palm trees,
and towards remote banks.

4
Under the bar's ceiling,
I drink a toast for the absentees and the
Deserted seats,
I drink a toast for a distant woman.
Oh, water lilies! Dreaming of accompanying,
The current,
We remain bound up to the bank all our lives.

Leave Me Alone

1
Leave me alone, I am worn out.
One by one they come,
The earth's sad ones,
And I have nothing other than my heart's fires
And the flower's weeping.

2
On the night of the stone woods, we wept
We were exchanging our childhood dreams,
We made the dreams pillows to sleep on.

3
"Leave me off"
I pierced far into your jungles,
But lost the way to the river
And the woods,
And the course of the village moon fringed,
With our young woman's hair
"You over there! I am worn out."
Every morning my heart's entrances,
Receive a woman visitor
And see another one off,
Leave me off.
Lean is my soul
And skinny is my body.

4
In privacy, I scream
Your lips are so remote,
Your hair is so enjoyable
When I take it by surprise,
I turn into a sail frustrated by wind.

When the Sea Falls in Love

1
When the losing journey tires you,
You sit down alone
To sip your bitter coffee, or to cry
Why did you choose for yourself this
Heathen journey,
Since you were not a god
Nor a demi-god.

2
Where will you go?
You had thought her island was good,
For rambling.
And its shores were smaller than a
Ploughed field,
To carry on your fingers to wherever
You like,
Did the fatal journey to the edge of her beauty
Not tire you?

3
Have you ever seen the trees run
Behind leaves?
Have you ever seen the deserted roads?

4
How will you pass over to the shores
Of the woman
Who has stolen your calmness?

5
Oh, Woman!
Whose love was like summer rain,
Or rainless colds,
Why did you allure this man who penetrated,
Deep into the woods of his misery
And the torture of his love?

6
A long time has since elapsed,
Yet you keep resisting
Your death in the risky rivers,
In the twilight of woods,
In a woman's face
That invited you to itself,
Then left spreading worldwide.

7
Oh, Charmer!
Washed in sadness,
In dust of exhausted cities,
This man who penetrated deep into the
Woods of his misery had loved you,
Then lost his childhood across the paths of
The forlorn night
And the lustre of two clear eyes.

8
Is this your face?
How can I gaze at its two banks
And not weep?
Had the sea been in love like you
When you descended into it,
It was sad,
It was talking about a seagull with
The colour of white foam.

9
Does this sea love its seagulls?
It remains sad
When the seagulls migrate in the
Dusk of the cold night,
All over the earth.

10
I remember your days,
The colour of your earlier childhood,
You warned me not to drink impure water
Nor to accompany a splintered moon.

11
You warned me
Not to give to the night, the sweetness
Of my voice,
Nor the cleanliness of my heart.
Why then do you give your footsteps
To a woman's pathway,
A woman who knows how to flirt with her lover
And to kill once she becomes too fed up?

12
You were a rainless cloud.
He was traveling to you foodless,
And waterless
You had thought he was an idol.

Shahryar the Peasant Dances Alone

Lonely, I cross the first distance
With the face of Shahryar, the bloody king
And the heart of a peasant from the south,
Where the sun passes while among us,
Leaving its light unto us,
As does Scheherazade's hair, leaving its
Fragrance on earth,
On the eve of the harvest.

"Shahryar!"
You are my face that remains held high
Whereas other faces humbly bend,
Down to earth.
The southern peasant entrusted me with their heart,
Here I am alone crossing the first distance,
Scheherazade is a woman who
Likes the goodness of Shahryar,
When dozing on her arm,
And Scheherazade weeps when he returns sad at midnight
On his lips, the smell of wine,
And on his rustic hair, a drop of dew.

This rustic king forgets not the brother of
His old torment,
Nor does he sell his earliest memories,
Since he loves your eyes as the poor love God,
He too loves the northern wind in the
Summer nights,
This rustic king has learned
To dance to the rhythm of the bank's ripples
Or the feast's tambourines,
Where you undo your hair tinged with henna
Into the wind and sing.

Oh, palm trees!
Abandon your position at the bank toward
The water
And let rivers wash your thin branches.
The girls celebrating the feast have come
Like cranes
To wash themselves and be rid of the,
Night's dust.

Shahryar knew not to betray his friends,
Nor to fuss about rituals.
A defect of his was to weep like a child
Deserted by woman
Or remembering his mother's bread
In the morning
So, he remains away,
Wandering in the charmed and blind city
In search of a little fragment of one night,
Of the thousand nights,
But soon they cut off his hand.

In the night's hiding place,
I carry his rustic sadness.
Where jazz revels
And the crazy waltz becomes louder
Scheherazade keeps aloof,
Or becomes part of the property of the
Well-to-do man.
Scheherazade, tonight I cozy up to the
Remotest, most deserted banquet
Why then on earth does Shahryar
Not kill himself?
The woman in the village usually has,
Your pure face
And the rustle of your muslin dress
When crossing the wheat field in midday.

Shahryar,
Maybe you would take off your summer moon-
Threaded garment and slip into darkness,
Maybe the beautiful face of our Scheherazade,
The peasant,
Would weep for you.
Over your hut, lying beyond a small height,
There.
Dreams do crowd.

The Wind was Southward

The heart's yearnings pass southward.
All rivers run southward,
The herds of tired stars come down southward
In search of a palm tree's trunk,
Fresh ripe dates and rains.

Under the shadow of leafing trees
Or between groves,
A peasant at his moment of rest sighs
And then sings
Glad tidings,
The mud-made cemetery won't receive
Our offspring this year.

Set your fire.
Hand me the tobacco pouch,
The wind is blowing southward.
Tonight, the clouds will shed tears at the wedding
Party of our stones,
Till their lashes cleave.

Do you remember the village's joy, the
Wind blowing southward?
These are dusty cities
The night becomes delightful,
We guffaw as the droplets of warm rain,
Pierce the hut's roof
And drop on our pillows.

The last bus will be leaving soon,
Empty your glass.
How happy the village is,
It brings out all its supply:
Loaves, remnants of dates, and
Jars of oil.

Southward the wreaths of flowers
Race together,
So do the birds of passage
And the swarms of branches
Southward, my voice travels every evening.

I don't know how the world would be
Without the woman I love
And without the south I bear,
In my travels across the territories of Cosmos.

The Castle

"Oh, door! If I had learned what would become of me
and what disasters your beauty would fetch me,
then I would have raised up an axe and smashed,
you and made a Kalak[1] out of you."
— Enkidu

1
Slow down,
Oh, streets whirling me from night to night!
I want to lean this tired body on one of
those walls,
Perhaps from its holes the mermaid may
Come out,
Abandoning it to drown in its griefs
She may undo her hair
And wrap the sailor with her braid.

2
It's the siege.
A castle ends up within a castle,
A wall within a wall,
A district with a muddy marsh
How can I recover my feet when they are sinking into
The asphalt of these wild streets?

---

[1] A flat type of boat usually needs used in rivers, especially between Baghdad and Samara, for carrying goods.

3
In these territories
I look for someone to crush the stones
That grow on my fingers,
Like the moss intertwining round the
thin stem of a flower.
Oh, Night! On which I started the time,
For travel.

4
Staying away from the meekness of huts,
I wish you wouldn't enjoy the delight
Caused by the north wind blowing
Upon you.
I wish no clouds would come to you
At the time of sowing stars in your,
snowy night.

5
There is no way before the strange
Bird, save death.
The woman could not prevent his face to age,
Nor his heart to grow old.
The bars couldn't protect him from grief,
The taste of bread has become like the
Taste of oleander
And laughing has become merely
The rustling of dry leaves,
Trodden by feet.

6
Slow down
Oh, mad streets!
I get tired of you.
It is dizziness that defiles what is left,
Of the bough's freshness
The road leading to the village we like
Has become farther,
So have the most beautiful women.
Formerly the fair wheat field had existed,
Before our flocks of birds,
Now it has moved and
We cannot reach it before nightfall.

Children and Gypsies

1
They come
And set their tents near the villages,
The women shout:
"The robbers of children, jewelry and,
Dresses have come."
The coming gypsies expose their women
For sale,
For the sake of bread
And drink wine twice a day,
Then sleep on beds of dust.

2
How much I loved the gypsies who were
Setting up their tents near the villages,
I loved the sadness
In their eyes, I loved the wings of department.
They were seeking an island, out of
Reach of Tatars.

3
I was weeping,
While mother cared to hold me tight
Behind her
And to press me to the hut's mat, which was
Smoke-coated by the winter brasier.
"Mother, I love them."
"Be careful not to say this
And make a dummy out of yourself
For their children to play with."

4
Oh, Children!
When the picaroon gypsies come
Back again,
Do not hide behind your mothers
And keep company with them.
Wherever their footsteps flogged by,
Winds take them
Perhaps there still is on this earth a span
Without wounds.

The Herb

Oh, Herb of the banks!
Is this my blood that travels in the body,
Or is it your river's silt that I drank
As a child?
And it remained stuck to my lips,
Like the taste of the first kiss,
And the prick of the first thorn,
And the love of the first woman
Who would part with us,
Or kill me
So that I rest
By no longer taking your face in my arms,
Overblown with dryness.

Stone Resurrection

1
Sitting here, who are you waiting for?
Staring at the bird returning from its migration,
The far horizon
You are going deeply into death,
Neither verse nor love overtakes you.
Who do you now wait for?
The orchards had collected their
Crumblings.
And what is left of the loving
Inscriptions on their trunks?
Then they spread out in the bleak snow.

2
Yesterday,
When rain sprinkled you,
You hung your expressionless face on
Abu Nuwwas'[2] face,
Asking him for some love,
For a drop from his glass.
When you wept, he kept silent?
He dried up your eyes with his
Stone garment.

---

[2] A Medieval Arab poet whose poems were known for their preoccupation with the consumption wine.

3
You will no longer fear to get wet,
Nor to catch cold,
Nor to be deprived of the shadow of trees
Thus, you keep standing under his silence
Waiting for the resurrection of stones
Whose theme was mainly on wine.

Away from Heaven

1
The soothsayer said,
"A wild time is squatting at the entrances
Of life,
Waiting for me
To have feathers on and a capable wing,
Waiting for me
To have two feet worthy of this earth,
To make us remain away from,
One another."

2
When your love grows branches
And blossoms,
I go out wafting like a summer's air
To meet tired generations.
Sad and alienated people
And parentless children,
To embrace them
And kiss the flowers of their childhood,
While weeping.

3
Who has distanced earth away from me?
Who has distanced me away
From your heaven?
Who has distanced the river away
From its banks?
And the trees from their birds?
Who has distanced the cloud away
From the sea?
And the lip from the mouth?

4
I shouldn't have wept all my life long,
Had your love's island not
Gone away from me.

The Awaited Woman

1
Before your love touched me,
I had the pride of palm trees
On whose age-old trunks, the
Night was pouring down.
I also had the patient foot whose
Wound fraternized
Between the stones of earth
And the deep cuts of the foot.

2
Leave a clue that guides me to you,
The shepherds escaped from me
Though I had been one of them.
A woman charmed my well-chosen, friend
And brought him to an end,
Was death a female?
She used to slip off her clothes and entice us,
But once we attempted to embrace her
She turned into a bird
Who neither vanished nor perched,
On age's bough.

3
It is evening,
The night is long; at the extreme end,
Of earth, it is ice.
I feel so tired,
Neither the mistress of the tavern,[3]
Opens the doors,
Nor does the vessel give me a lift
To the master of flood[4]
Or to kingdom of reeds.

---

[3] Siduri who Gilgamesh asked to guide him to Utanapishtim
[4] Utanapishtim himself in the legend of Gilgamesh

What is Left of the Happy Time?

1
Count your inheritances
Or reread your old notebooks,
Since your feet touched the thorns of earth
You learnt nothing but painful names.

2
Far from you is the sky of the first laugh
And your first love, and the roofs.
Now penetrate deep into the regions of fears.

3
Oh, woman!
The one you have awaited is no longer
Fit for love or singing,
Leave!
And accompany your green star.

4
What has been left of your happy time
Is no more than an aged youthful woman,
A woman your hand had neither touched,
Nor on her bosom had you rested your
Murdered dreams.

5
What has been left.
It's no more than just straws of memories
That you carried
And roamed the earth with,
Your back bent,
Your body soaked to the bone.
You forgot
That the death of those ages
Will always remain, without resurrection
The tambourine you had saved for,
Felt worn out
And the henna was spilt.

6
Don't sing.
Your voice is no longer laden with wheat,
Nor the flutter of the evening bird's wing,
Nor the braids of the woman you loved,
Don't sing!
Sobbing roars in your voice
And crying blows like wind.

7
Count your inheritances.
The last one abandoned you, returned naked
Having nothing but sadness
And his shabby clothes.
You may see him dance,
Hear him sing
But this is the last elegy.
Those who died were countless,
The loneliness of walls is unbearable.
So, save the remainder of love
For that babe who will see the,
Light one day.

The Friends

1
At night, my soul yearns for you.
Two wings of loneliness grow in the heart.
What a bird, this heart of mine!
What if you doze?
And on the pillow of my eyelids, you rest
Your wings.

2
What if you block the bay of your yearning
And keep the faces of your beloved away?
You're taking a risk,
Neither the sea,
Nor the back of the tired wind
Knows where the sad people of this
Exile reside.

3
Tonight, I remember you all,
The trumpets of sadness sound loud,
So do the flutes of alienation.

4
Oh, the whole birds of tears!
Oh, my sweetheart! Crowd before,
My blood's ash,
Collect the feathers. Oh, Me!
And the boughs of hair;
Pretty I was.

5
Appease my heart's fears
And bear my sobbing,
I have.

6
Who was as thin as a herb?
And as skinny as a lover's body
To summon them in the quiet of the night
But I heard no voice except mine?

For All the Things I Love

1
For the sake of this word's griefs, I grieve.
For the sake of children's survival, I sing.
For the sake of my southern deserted fields,
I search for my severed hand and an ax.
And for the sake of a woman, I will die.

2
The world is running towards rocky slopes
I am the herb
I am the wind coming late at night,
Moist with dew and slumber,
How can I stop?

3
This mad one is running towards its end,
I have no weapons.
Would I tie it to the tender herbs,
To the broken waves of the bank,
And to the coolness of the night's moon?

4
Wild and fearful I know this world
I said to it,
Oh, crazy world running towards your end!
Shake off from your body the cement,
The deadly atomic dust
And the blackness of tar.
It turned its back on me
And resumed the game of snipping the
Necks of flowers.

Fields of Winter Days

1
Every morning my woman and my
Six children
Stare at my face.

2
This woman is good hearted,
Every morning she holds the kitchen knife
And slices the years of lifetime
And cooks them for me.

3
Between the kitchen and the ferocity of
My agonies she moves silently,
She does not weep;
This makes me dream of other mornings.

4
The lucky patients like me are only few,
No one feels disgust towards me,
This may occur later on,
But now
At the peep of every day,
My mother's lips start to repeat one,
Of the village prayers
My mother knows
That the villagers' prayer is closest to,
Allah's[5] heart.

5
On some days, I remain tied to my bed;
This hurts me.
Outside my bedroom I have my own,
Good things,
How I desire to accompany them,
In my wanderings.

6
I mostly like the winter days
People fear the winter days,
I alone adore them.

---

[5] Allah means God

7
Over there, are the drizzles of quiet rain,
The bluish misty mornings,
The little clouds like the alert of
A heart for a long journey
And the flocks of birds return from,
Their migration.
8
A lot of things I may relish during winter days,
To escort a woman in good walks
And to start flirting with her under
The soft drizzle.
The winter days are the year's gift for me,
They give toys to my life's childhood
And fill my pockets with flowers,
Similar to the growing ones among the,
Wheat fields,
Together with my girlfriends' photos.

9
The winter days sadden my woman,
She is goodhearted,
This I don't deny,
But she does not stand drawing out of my pocket;
A woman's photo,
Her letters,
A tuft of hair,
Or some withered flowers.

10
My woman, the peasant, knows
I can't live without her loving,
Nor without my girlfriends' flowers.
She doesn't shout in my face,
All she does is look sad,
I know that I don't take the object of
My girlfriends away from her.

11
So, when coming home,
I bashfully nod before her blues,
Take her rough hands
And kiss the traces of the kitchen knives
And what is left by the hoofs of years,
Like a child infuriated his parents,
I ask her for forgiveness
And she forgives me.

12
The lucky patients like me are only few,
Up to this moment.
I still practice my daily walks
And I recall the rainy years.

13
The cattle wandering down the meadows,
The friends,
Some of them abandoned me,
Few of them still come up to me,
And weep before me.
In this heartless time how happy you are to meet
One who asks after you.

The Pasture's Days

1
Bare feet,
Storks picking up the cow's worms,
Soft lands
And singing, stealing away from the,
Remote reed thickets:
Those were the kingdoms of my
First pasture.

2
What a child!
A lark built a nest on my soul's harbour,
The satanic play of lambs appealed
To me
And the pasture's fairies made
Me their son.

3
Every autumn,
The trees dress their shoulders with
Yellowish gowns,
The river stops bearing its canoes.

4
I try to doze, but
A day before the pasture's fairies took,
me out to dry brooks,
There they exchanged making love to me.

5
How I wish to doze
And dream of the braids of the
Pasture's fairies,
With herb-like fragrance,
But my father's hand wakened me,
The bell was about to announce the,
Start of the lesson.

6
On the way to the village school
I looked up at the chilly horizon,
I see white-fringed clouds run fast,
I know the rainy season will shortly come,
I begin gathering the shadow of trees.

7
The songs of woman wood-cutters,
The bleat of sheep,
The smell of the ploughed soil;
Suddenly, I tear the lesson's copybook up.

8
To the wild thickets,
The shepherdess took me,
Spread her braid on me,
Drew my face close to her lips;
She taught me how to embrace her and to sleep.

9
I don't know how my father's hand
Groped my ripped feet.
The lightening retreating eastward
Was overflowing the entire hut,
I looked at that exhausted face, my father's face,
That face was sadly reproaching me.

10
At daybreak of the next day,
The shepherdess were searching for
A flock of shags,
And I was plunging my body into
The pools of paper.

The Children of My Country

1
You, children of my country,
Were once the earth,
As good as Mom's breast
And hot bread.

2
When spring, with rich greenness, comes,
You collect the wild flowers
And race behind the butterflies,
Often the wet dawn washes
Your little feet.

3
You liked to play under the shadows
Of densely leafed trees.
In the hot summer noon,
The river took to embracing you
As if it were a dally.

4
Oh, children!
Children of my country,
Where sun no longer rises,
Nor Spring pays a visit.

5
Lifeless, your joys are,
Like boatless shores
Where no seagulls tread,
The sand.

6
At daybreak,
Dimness still envelopes the
Tree tops
As pale as the faces of invalids.

7
At this time,
The heartbroken moms wake you up
To go to school, as the world's children do.
But alas! Instead, you go either digging,
In the piles of litter
Or begging at the traffic lights.

8
You, children of my country!
You sell your childhood for stale bread
And empty rusty cans.
Let me hold your light in my hands,
And cry.

9
You've forgotten the names of your schools,
You've forgotten the moments of,
Innocent fun.
The hardest thing,
You've forgotten you're still children.

10
The tombs now give birth to your twins,
Famine is choked with its fatness as it
Gulps your thin bodies.
In your sleepless eyes
Sadness swells up
With wild settlement.

11
You good little sparrows,
I bow before you,
Like a saint before the Lord,
And ask you to save the children of my
Country with your red bills.

12
They're light and thin
Like thin straws.
If you brought them back,
With their violated smiles,
You could build their dreams
And make the world's mornings
A little brighter,
While listening to their childish
And friendly songs.

Forests of the Night

While behind the door,
Listening to footsteps crossing the street,
from one side to another,
I remember that night,
Those wet pavements
And them.

Those pavements will no longer
Receive us.

Night woods
Resembled a sun-bathed field.
We set out to cross them from end to end.

Did those forests light up?
Or were we too tipsy to see
The distinction between light and dark?

They were like me
The night brought back to them the
Memory of the forgotten days,
Chasing her down roads,
Once she got tired
He gripped the ends of her mantle and,
Pushed her into the house.

In the last stage of our journey
The wet roads appealed to us.

At this bar
We drink mugs of beer,
At that cafe
We drink cups of tea.

Now and then we become tipsy.
We lose our way home,
But we've never lost the way to
The woman.

In moments of drunkenness,
I become heavy and weary,
I weep inside the bus;
So do all the tipsy ones.

My friends tolerate my weeping,
I take them wherever I like,
They make no protest.

Quite often I stopped them against,
A building.
One evening,
A woman offered to grant me the
Blessing of her love,
But I heeded not to that woman's love.
My friends bore the fault of the situation.

My friends are a rare host,
They don't belong to this era,
My memory refuses to abandon them.

It's hard to shun a woman's heart,
To listen to the songs of ducks
And to the rustle of the night wind.

It's hard to remember some friends
With whom you went to a bar or a café,
To laugh or to weep.
Yet, you are requested not to grieve.

It's No Use for Me to Dream

1
I shook off my last dream,
Why should I dream
As long as I sit on heaps of corpses,
of dreams?

2
We'll become reconciled, the
World and I. It's funny
For a lamb to quarrel with a pasture wolf.

3
Nobody can weep
As much as I can.

4
I loved as many women as the heart's wounds.
Those wounds ran countless.

5
The death of my day worries me.
I wish it would not have pain;
Its flower would lie calmly.

6
I promise you,
I will care for the problem of my village smell,
My smell resembles the smell of my cows.

7
Inside my heart there is more than
One shelter.
For the village memories,
There I will hide her.

8
Once I remove that smell from my
Body, I'll grieve.

9
No crazy one ever born will be satisfied
With hunger, but me.

10
I said to the sparrow of dawn,
Don't be ashamed of touching the night's feet
There the grains of wheat
And the nests of warmth lurk.

11
I assure you all, I trained my fancies,
If there will ever be a madman concerned
With my affair,
He need not worry for me.

12
I won't dream of living near the sea,
Nor building a resort for my nerves.

13
I have no problem.
The last thing I do before passing,
Away is
To knock at a woman's door.

14
That woman won't rebuke me
If I ask her for some food,
She'll offer me the rose of her lips.

Let Us Go Beg Together

1
Like a lily, a current swept away,
Like a short of cloud, wind snatched,
Like a sparrow the mid-summer obliged
To seek shelter in the shadow,
Come on.

2
Without your hair as my pillow,
The days are only desolate woods.

3
The muddy roads
Are of no use for the embrace
Between two persons resembling us.
We are clean enough to vex
This marsh.

4
Sweet things never survive in the
Earth for long;
Neither do the rivers,
Nor the parents,
Nor the heart's joy,
Nor you.

5
I need someone to convince me
That the blissful time took flight.

6
Children lost the branch
Of their childhood.
Your hair altered its wheaten colour.

7
I need someone to convince me
I am no longer a child toying
With your braids.

8
Come on, let's beg for some of the
Flower's fragrance,
Some of the scent of bygone days.

God Will Not Descend Again

1
You won't see the good Lord,
Lord of the plant offshoots,
Of cattle pastures
And of the peasants' songs during the
Season of wheat harvest.

2
That Lord,
With pastoral scent,
Won't descend again.
Leprous cities
Welcome none save Satan.

3
Nothing is clean in this world,
So, apologize to your Lord for the
death of our joy.

4
Both our hearts are desolate shores,
Allah has abandoned them.

Birds Travel Far Away

1
Like a shadow of a cloud, the year passes.
Once I lift up my head to see it,
It shakes off the feathers of its wings
And passes.

2
You are white
Like white threads,
Clinging to the huts of peasants,
Bringing good news that a winter's
Rainy evening is coming.

3
Between the woods' winter and the,
Farm's autumn,
I look for you.
Withered leaves drop upon my
Clothes
And the remnants of the stiff grass
Make my feet bleed.

4
Across the heart's wildernesses,
I glimpse flocks of birds going to and fro,
But you
Reside far away.

5
Thirsty sparrows,
Leafless trees,
Steppes on which no herds of
Dreams graze,
Are the kingdoms where I now mount
The throne.

6
My fingers are no longer supple,
One day
They were your most beautiful combs,
Nothing but my fingers had delighted,
Your hair.
But now,
I see them busy driving my years away,
Those years shade my window
Like dark blinds.
I open them slightly, a little wider,
Just to see you.

The Tree

To my Mother

1
You were a little kid,
The night rains soaked into your bed,
You screamed.
The cold agonized you, you screamed.

2
You were emaciated like the village shanties,
like bare trees,
Like a path untrodden by a woman
In which the heaps of wheat did not
lean waist to waist.

3
Do you scream?
You were little kid,
Her hands fumbled your head
And your woolen cap.

4
She knows the secret of your screaming,
But
Do you know why you are screaming
Tonight?

5
You were far away,
And the remnants of her hand's warmth were
The last things you carry in your travels
Whenever you listen to the furious rain
Or recall a little child held in her arms,
While crossing the village paths and singing
"Oh, My lady al-Zahra!
Take your pretty son,
Perhaps in the morning he will be
Trodden
By horses' hoofs."

6
Were you tonight
To remember the colour of her plait,
Her warm hand-made bread,
Her mantle's rustle,
While sprinting under the furious rain,
Lest your clothes might not get wet.

Ah, I wish you had not known that the
World was larger than you had thought
Ah, I wish you had not known the grief.

8
When frost drops down the roads
And the wind whistles,
Remember that another woman
Had granted you her plaits,
The wound illuminated.

The River

1
Tonight, we commence our dialogue in silence,
The latest river passed us alienated.
It had left behind its two banks running
On the dryness of earth.
They both asked every passerby about the,
Departure of trees.

2
The room becomes gloomy,
This is not the time for you to sleep.
Take off sleep from your lasher,
This man who suffers from torture's stab
Desires you to be the final date-palm at the
Boundary between the river and the desert
And the final haven towards which the
Journey sets out.

3
Do you have anything which makes
Silence less lonely
And brings me closer to your delicious hell?
The little ones dream,
You dream of dancing with date-palms at
The moment of their being replete with spate
And of washing your hair at the spring.

4
You fear the tale of departure.
Open the windows,
The air is not ruthless
At such a time of March.

5
You took to leave our shanty and head
For the river.
The season of harvest was striding across
The field of wheat laughing.
The innocent moon was bathing in your
Eyes twice a day.

6
The final goblet sticks out from both my hands
And you are at the remotest corner
Gazing at both, the time's face lurking
In your eyes
And the wild lilies.

I Need You

1
I need your voice,
Your voice is a rare thing.
Since the village time,
I haven't washed my eyes with it.

2
This vast silence
Causes me fear and loneliness
And reminds me of stars over there.
They only rise from your lips.

3
Oh footsteps!
Pass swiftly
And be careful not to leave a trace
On the shore.

4
In more than one winter resort,
I have looked for your warmth,
This chill keeps on peeling my bones.

5
My fear reached its peak.
I haven't prepared yet,
I have no travel kit,
My way towards your time is
Extremely long.

6
From their highest top the days roll down
To the foot,
With them I also slip down.

7
As the cold wind passes,
I stand waiting.
How fierce this wind is!

8
When cold becomes more intense
I dream of a garment like your hair.

9
Your hair is a warm season,
The floods of pasture.
What a good companion your hair was!

10
It's not possible
For me to run down like dewdrops
And for your lips not to cling onto me.

11
There is a song,
If we listen to its sweetness
We cease being sad.
The lost dreams are too many
To be counted.

12
One of my errors was
I made you stand sparkling in the sun.

13
Since the dryness of the moonshine's lakes,
We haven't seen each other.

14
Not to meet again
Means one thing.
The night storm has driven your birds away.

Primitive Love Rituals

1
Once a waft of fragrance reaches me
From afar,
The river of my blood runs fast
To meet you,
My lashes run fast to embrace you
And my heart hugs yours.

2
Once I thirst,
Your lips change into rivers.
Once I hunger,
Your song becomes my banquet.

3
Charmer you are,
Up to this moment I still keep touching
My pulse.
A song overtakes me,
Advising me not to grieve
And encouraging my dreams not
To age.

4
My home, you are
Under the shadows of your boughs.

5
My midsummer splits asunder,
If I die,
I'll get up from my dead body
And reside on the shores of your lips
Till my destined Doomsday.

6
The most beautiful things I carry
While crossing this world
Are only some scare made by
Your kisses
The sweetest thing adorning my memory
Is only your sleep on my arm.

Crying

I desire to cry
Before the masses of the weary.
As a secret circular,
I insert into their hands some of
my dreams.

If I were left to choose
The manner of my death,
Your open arms are a very
Beautiful field
And upon its pillows I'll be dying.

Travelling was a dream of enjoyment,
But it has turned out to be an escape.

From this world I only ask for
a few sparrows.
Once I accost them
They don't take to flight
dreadfully.

Sparrows Of The Cities

With their soiled feathers,
And their beaks dirty with stagnant water,
The sparrows of the city wake up,
Lazy and exhausted.
Like the voices of drunken men,
And those who were tired,
Uttering a song, burdened with sorrow.

To that song,
The morning air groans.
The bows of the trees and
The eyes are terrified of
Another new day.

Not the rotten bread,
Not the convoys of nightmares,
Not the horrors that come over us,
As we become living creatures,
Tougher than their calamity.

Tonight Wake You With Roses

Tonight, we light a lamp, we come to you,
One by one, circling your pillow, watching
Flocks of ducks flying over your closed eyes
On their quick flight into exile.
What kind of drowsiness is breaking
Over your eyes,
Clear as spring water,
Calm as spring water,
Free-flowing as spring water?
What kind of drowsiness can this be
When flocks of ducks arrive
And fly away
And your sails do not depart?
We gather around you.
More rivers than one still trace a way
Between those lips, so speak to us.
Who told you the country moon would die,
The heart would die?
And the child of love would die?
Who told you seas abuse seagulls,
That the shore does not embrace each breaking wave,
Nor give shells to children?
No one told you.
The earth is your cloak of warmth in the rain,

The grass your sleeping place,
The hair of the women you've loved a pillow for your
Sleep.
You are time, water,
The kingdom,
So how could you die?
....

Translated by
Anne Fairbairn & Ghazi al — Gosaibi
Published in (Feathers and The Horizon)
Canberra (Australia): The Leros Press 1989

Anne Mary Ross Fairbairn AM (1928 — 22 October 2018)

Anne Mary Ross Fairbairn was a widely published Australian poet, journalist, and expert in Arab culture. She is the only granddaughter of Australia's fourth Prime Minister, George Reid.

Fairbairn has been known for her work in bringing together Australian and Arab cultures for over 30 years through poetry.

In 1995, she was awarded the Banjo Paterson Writing Award for Open Poetry. This was followed by the Order of Australia in 1998 for services to literature and international relations between Australia and the Middle East.

In September 2005 Dr. Fairbairn received the award, "Living for Others — Promoting Peace through Media, Arts and Culture" from the International and Inter-Religious Federation for World Peace presented in Sydney by Professor Marie Bashir AO, Governor of New South Wales. She died at the age of 90 on 22nd October 2018.

Ghazi Abdul Rahman Al Gosaibi (3 March 1940 — 15 August 2010)

Ghazi Abdul Rahman Al Gosaibi was a Saudi politician, diplomat, technocrat, poet, and novelist. He was an intellectual and a member of the Al Gosaibi family, one of the oldest and richest trading families of Saudi Arabia and Bahrain. Al Gosaibi was considered among Saudi Arabia's topmost technocrats since the mid-1970s. The Majalla called him the "Godfather of Renovation" while Saudi journalist Othman Al Omeir argued that he was "the only great man in Saudi Arabia".

Publications

Books
1 - *Passing to the Cities of Joy*, Iraq.1973
2 - *Chapters from The Journey of the Southern Bird*. Iraq, 1976
3 - *Southern Sky*. Iraq, 1979
4 - *Woman is My Kingdom*. Iraq, 1982
5 - *The Winter of Pastures*. Iraq, 1992
6 - *Silence of Huts*. Iraq,1996
7 - *I Call You from a Distant Place*. Egypt, 2008
8 — *Peace Be Upon You Mariam*. Amman, Jordan, 2012. ISBN: 9789957302924
9- *Ayam qarih almuhsanah* (Novel: The days of Muhssineh's village), Amman, Jordan, 2011. ISBN: 9789957302498
10 - *En kontinent av sång* (A continent of singing), translated into Swedish, by
Hasan Al-Yasiri and Anna-Maria Nilson, Qatar, 2013. ISBN 9789163731730
11- *The Complete Poems of Issa Hassan Al-Yasiri*. Beirut, Arab Institute for Research and Publishing 2017. ISBN : 978614419332
12- *Chants du Crépuscule* (Songs of the Twilight) translated into French by Monia Boulila, L'Harmattan, Paris, France, 2018. ISBN: 9782343153490
13- *Oración primitiva por URUK* (Primitive prayer for URUK) translated into Spanish by Ignacio Gutierrez de

Teran, Madrid, 2018. ISBN: 9788417707194

14- *Catedral de Bagdad Y otros poemas* (Baghdad Cathedral and other poems). translated into Spanish by Hasan Issa Al-Yasiri, Layla Fadhil, Faouzia Elkadiri, and Ignacio Gutierrez de Teran. Revised by Abdul Hadi Sadoun. Madrid: Olifante. Edicions de Poesia, 2020.

15- *Dias de la aldea de AL MUHSINA* (Novel: The days of Muhssineh's village). translated into Spanish by Noemi Fierro. Madrid: Editorial Verbum, 2020. ISBN: 9788413372891

16- *The Complete Poems of Issa Hassan Al-Yasiri*. Vol. 3. Beirut, Arab Institute for Research and Publishing, 2021 ISBN:9786144861707.

17- The Distant Land. Translated into English by Emeritus Professor Abdel-Wahid Muhammed, New York: Austin Macauley Publishers. 2021. ISBN: 9781647506124

18- Je *m'en vais seul* (I am going alone) from the publishing house (L'Harmattan) Paris. France 202. ISBN: 9782343204840.

Magazines

20- The Empty Chaires. A poem translated into English by the Australian poet Anne Fairburn (1928-2018). Voices Magazine. Australia. Winter 1993.

21- On the Banks of Your Rivers I Weep. A poem translated into English by Salih J. Altoma. Malpais Review. Autumn 2011. USA.

22- Baghdad's Cathedral Excerpts. A poem translated into English by Salih J. Altoma. Aljadid. Vol. 23. N.77. 2020. USA.

23- Soliloquy, The Pupil. Poems translated into English by

Abdel-Wahid Muhammed. The Voices of Rial 4: a poetry compilation book by various poets. 2020
24- A Primitive Prayer for Uruk. A poem translated into English by Ghareeb Iskander. Arabllit Quarterly. May 25, 2020. UK.

https://arablit.org/2020/05/25/lock-in-literature-a-primitive-prayer-for-uruk/?fbclid=IwAR3iKan4F8i12ZyI_iZNgWJfhCJf2Fzhv7cdq1drcTnZw088phA3OGZY4f4

Critical and Analytical Studies and articles about His Poetry

1. Ala' Mohsin Al-hassani. *'Issa Hassan Al-Yasiri's Poetry: An Artistic Study'*. Beirut, Arab Institute for Research and Publishing, 2019. ISBN: 9786144860182
2. Fatima Khalifa *"A basket of fruits"*. Doha: Defaf, 2013
3. Hussain Sarmak Hassan *"Issa Hassan Alyasiri: Village's Poet or Humanitarian's Poet"*.Amman: Dar Fadaat, 2012. ISBN : 9789957303778
4. Fatima Khalifa *"Fields of Issa Hassan Al-yasiri"* Lebanon, 2018. ISBN: 9786144199183
5. Altoma.Salih J. "The Herb: Selected Poems by Aisa Alyasiry (Isa Hasan Al-Yasiri), An Iraqi Canadian Poet". The Montréal Review, February 2012.
http://www.themontrealreview.com/2009/The-Herb-Selected-Poems-by-Aisa-Alyasiri.php
6. Abisaab, Rula Jurdi. The Death of Plows and Books: Isa al-Yasiri's Devastating Vision. of Peasant Migration from the Iraqi South. Aljadid. Vol.18. No. 67. 2013-2014. USA

7. Gregor Flakiersld. *"Poesi Med starkt diktarag"*. Tidningen Angermanland. 19 april 2014.
(This critical article published in Sweden based on his poetry collection *En kontinent av sång* (A continent of singing).
8. José Antonio Santano. La Semilla De Uruk (Uruk Seed). 05 novembre 2019
(This critical article published in Spain based on his long poem Oración primitiva por URUK (Primitive prayer for URUK).
9. Bertholom, Louis. Issa Hassan Al-Yasiri, d'Irak à Montréal (from Iraq to Montreal). Sepred Gouez: L'esprit sauvage. No. 26. 2020. France.

Anthologies:
1- Al-Muttalibi, Khaloud. *A Portrait of Uruk: an anthology of poems and stories*. London, 2011.203 p. (Aisa Hassan Al-Yassiri p.31-46) ISBN: 9781460981108
2- Al-Muttalibi, Khaloud. *The Contemporary Iraqi Poetry Movement: The Future of the Past*. London, 2012.113 p. (Aisa Hassan Al-Yassiri p.78-85). ISBN : 9780957290907
3- 3-Al-Toma Salih J. Iraq's Modern Arabic Literature: A guide to English Translations since 1950.Toronto, The scarecrow press.inc. 2010. 155 p. ISBN: 9780810877054
4- L'Anneau Poétique (Poetry group). Les Poètes dans le monde / Poets in the World. (Montréal) 2015. 70 p. (Aisa Hassan Al-Yassiri p.60-62). ISBN: 9780986657245

Festivals and conferences:
1- The World Goethe Festival Held in Democratic Germany on the 3rd of Oct. ,1975.

2- The Conference of the Arab Writers' Union held in Damscus on the 27th of Nov.,1979.
3- The Arab Poetry Festival held in Amman /Jordan on the 7th of Feb. 2000; on inaugurating the House of Poetry.
4- The International Festival of Poetry held in Rotterdam / Holland on the 25th of May 2002.
5- The Cultural Jithoor symposium held in Detroit/ USA in Winter, 2005.
The 32^d Edition of « Festival International de la Poésie » in Trois-Rivières, Québec, from 30 September to 9 October 2016

www.ingramcontent.com/pod-product-compliance
Lightning Source LLC
LaVergne TN
LVHW041536060526
838200LV00037B/1008